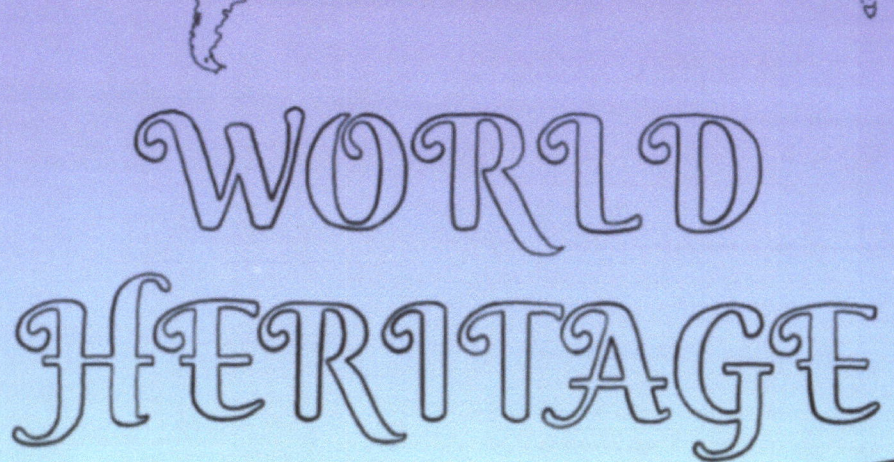

In a magical land lived a curious little girl named Laura. Laura loved to dress up in all sorts of costumes and pretended to be someone new each day. One day, Laura's grandmother handed her a beautiful scarf. "This scarf holds the magic of the world's costume heritage," her grandmother said. Excitingly, Laura wrapped the scarf around her shoulders and closed her eyes. Suddenly, she felt a gentle breeze carrying her away to far-off lands. First, Laura found herself in India. She was wearing a sari and dancing to the beat of a Bollywood song. Next, she was in Japan, dressed in a pretty kimono like a butterfly. Laura travelled the world, discovering the beauty and diversity of each culture's costume heritage. Laura returned home at sunset. Her heart was full of joy. She knew that her adventure had only begun. She realized that no matter where you go or what you wear, the magic of costume heritage is about celebrating who you are and where you come from.

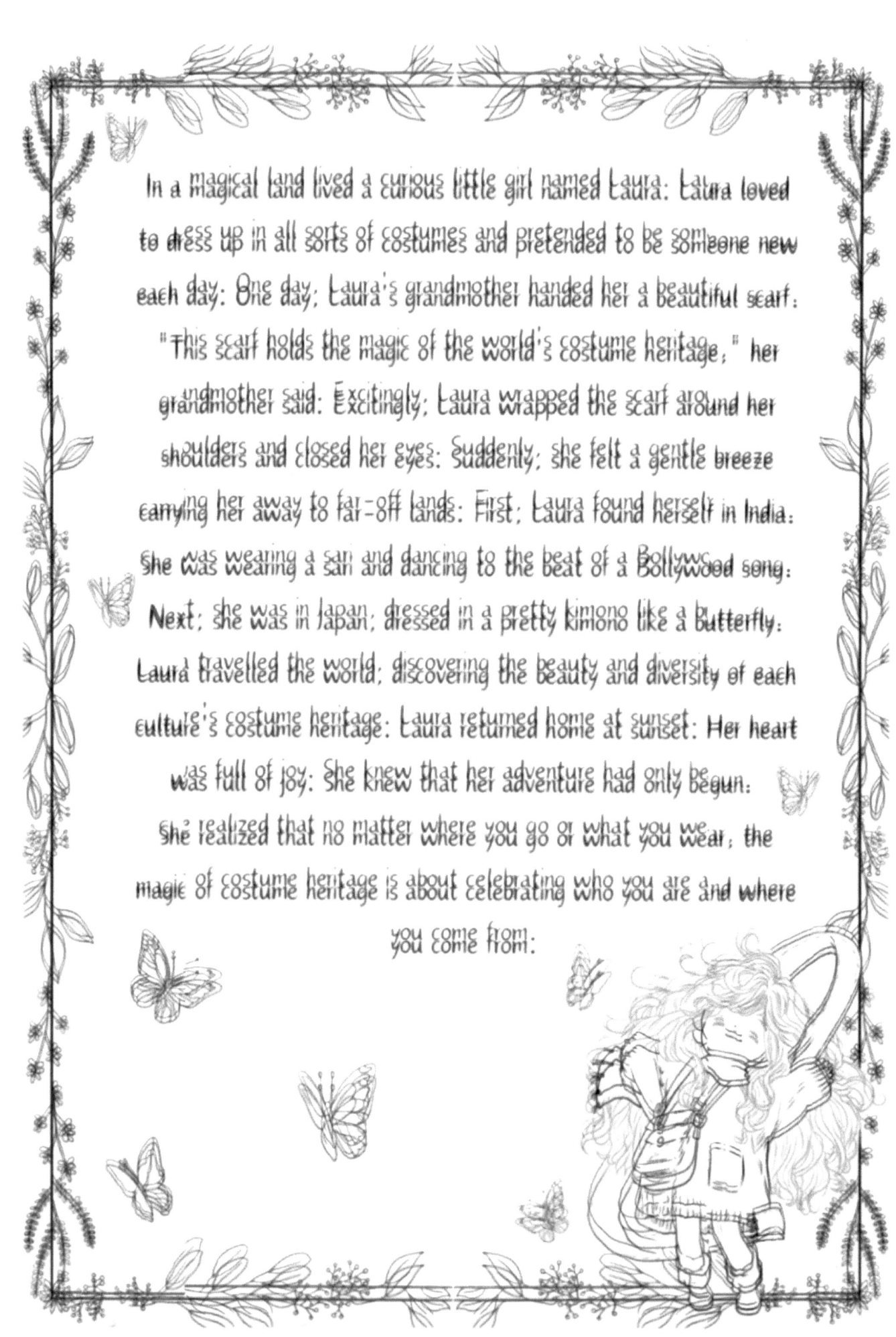

INDIA

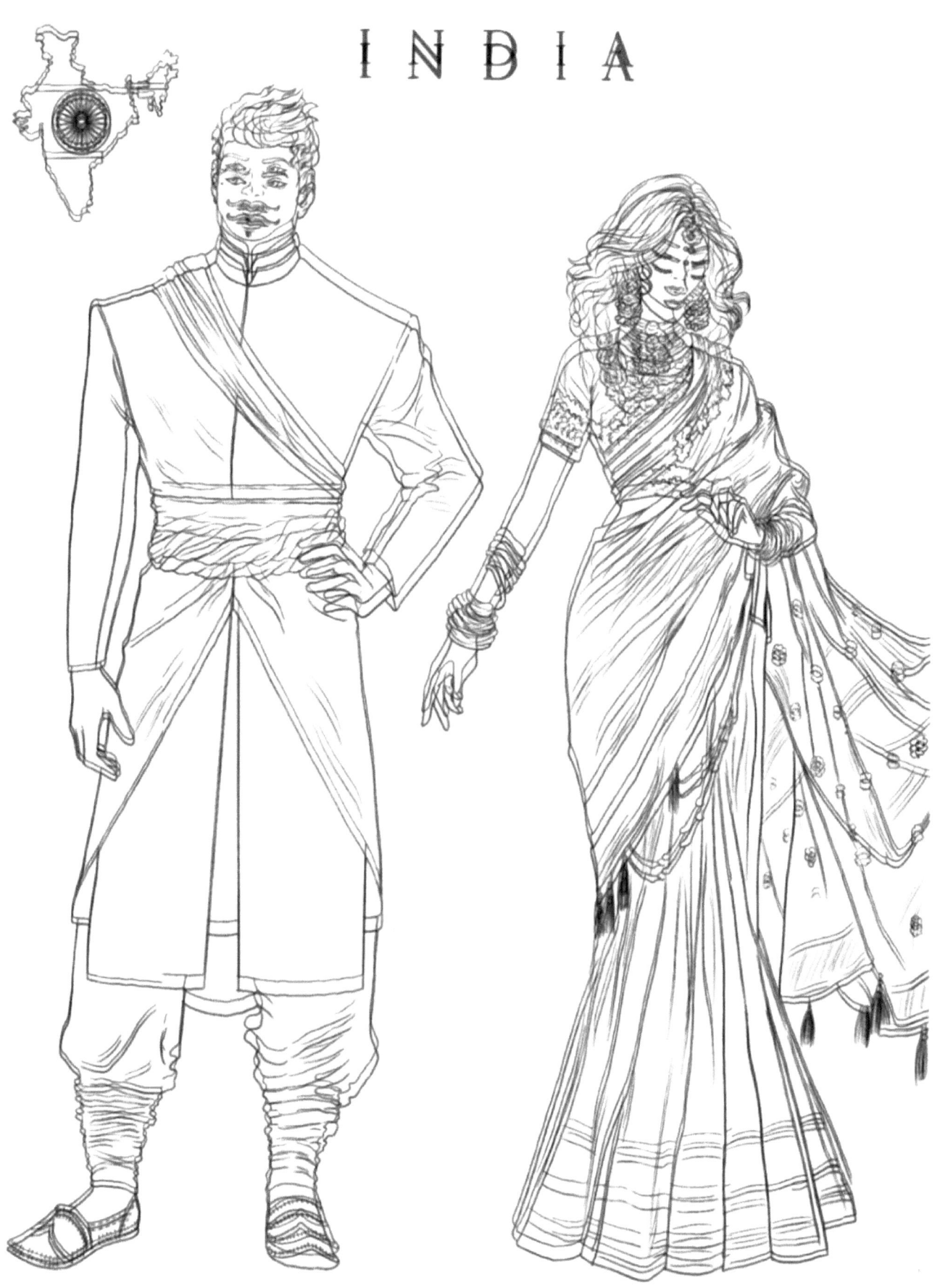

SOUTH KOREA

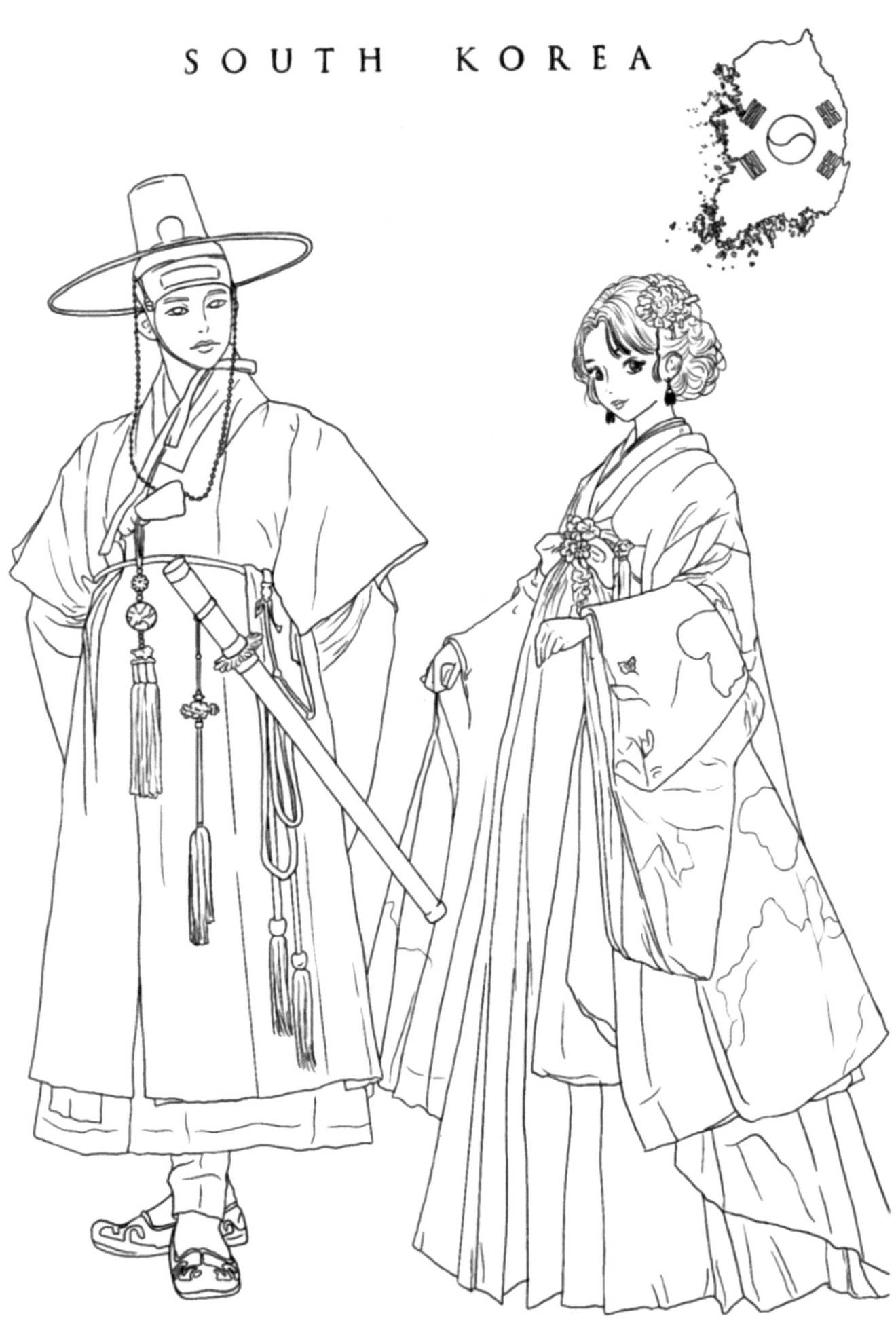

JAPAN

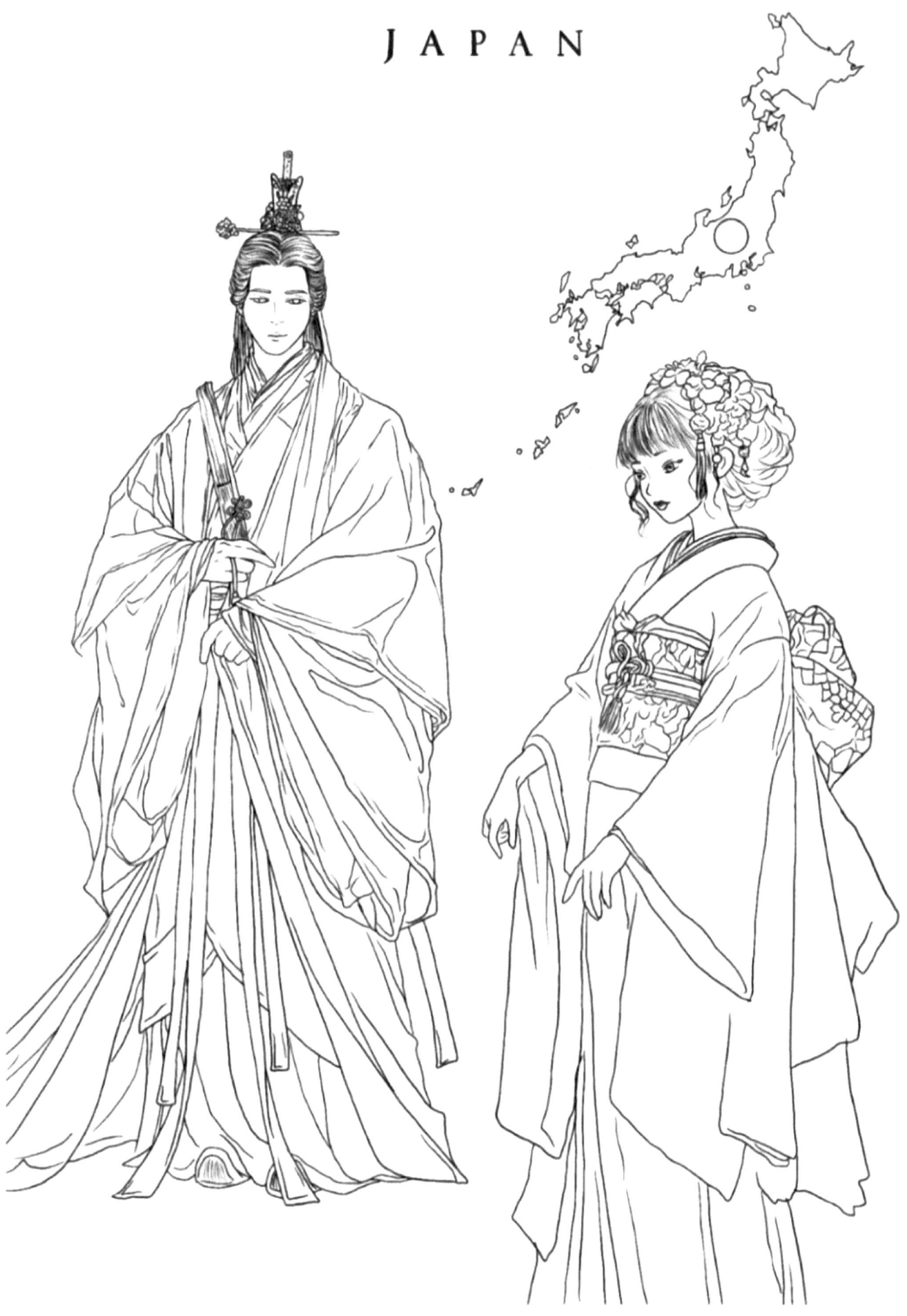

CIRCASSIAN

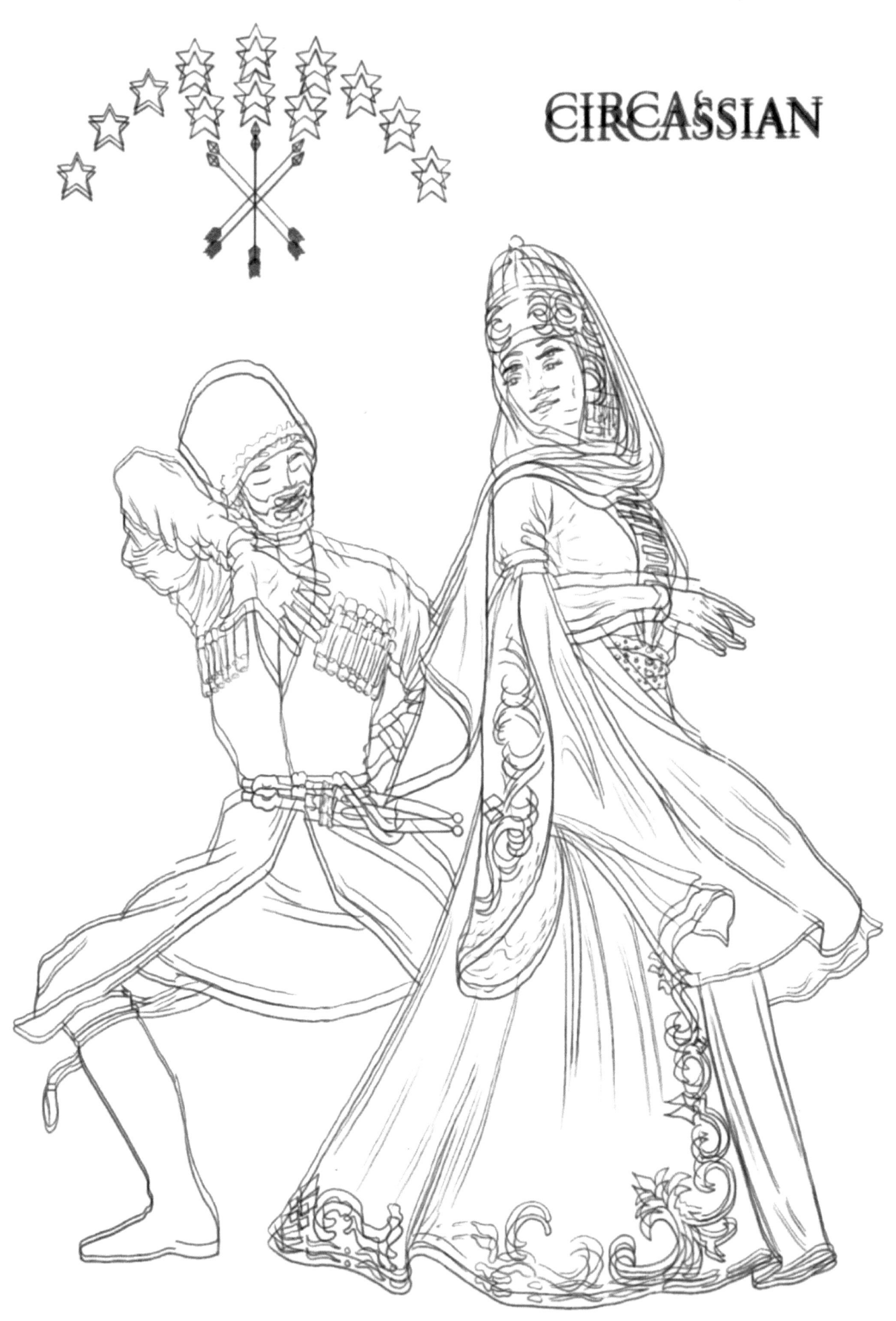

NORWAY

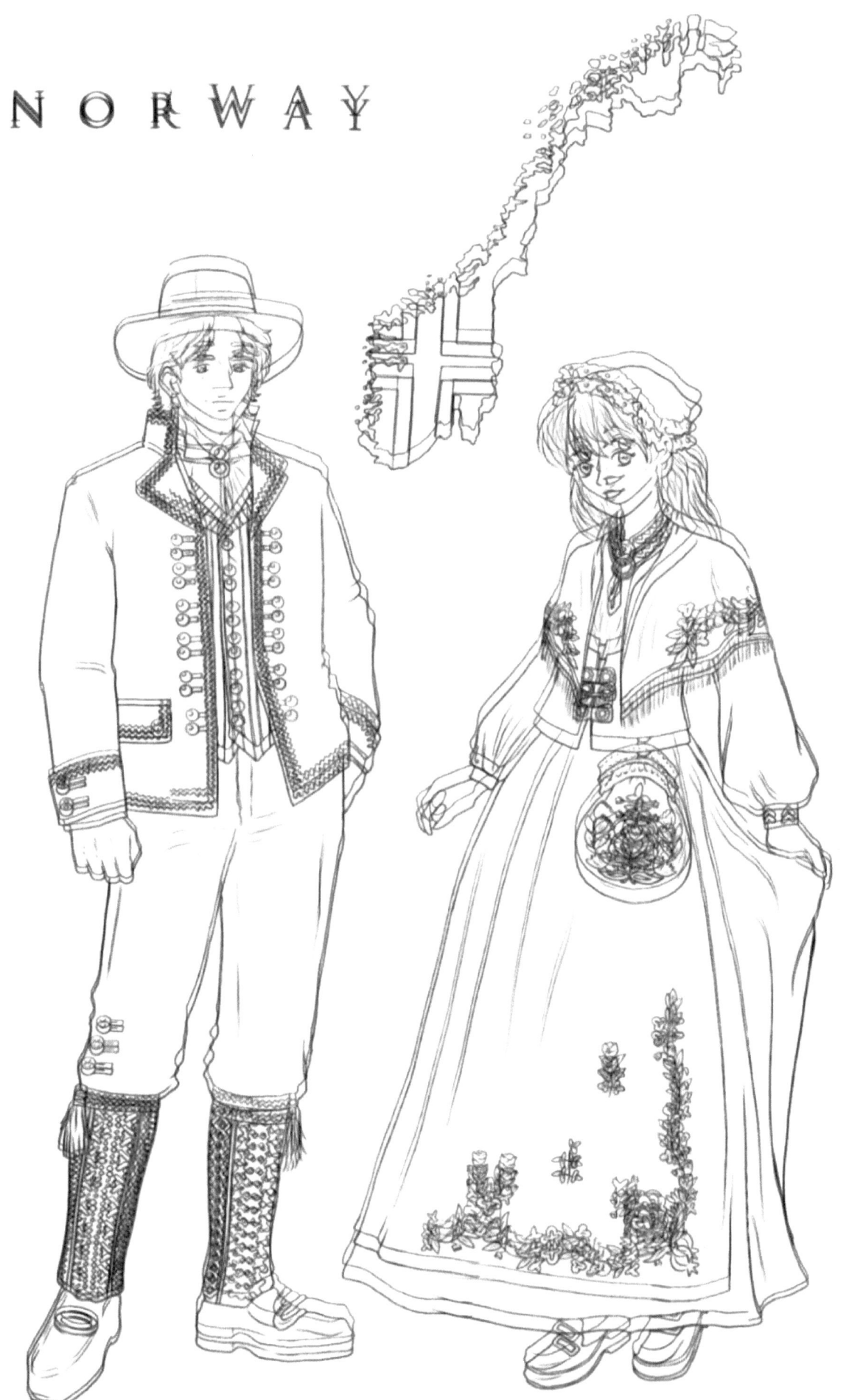

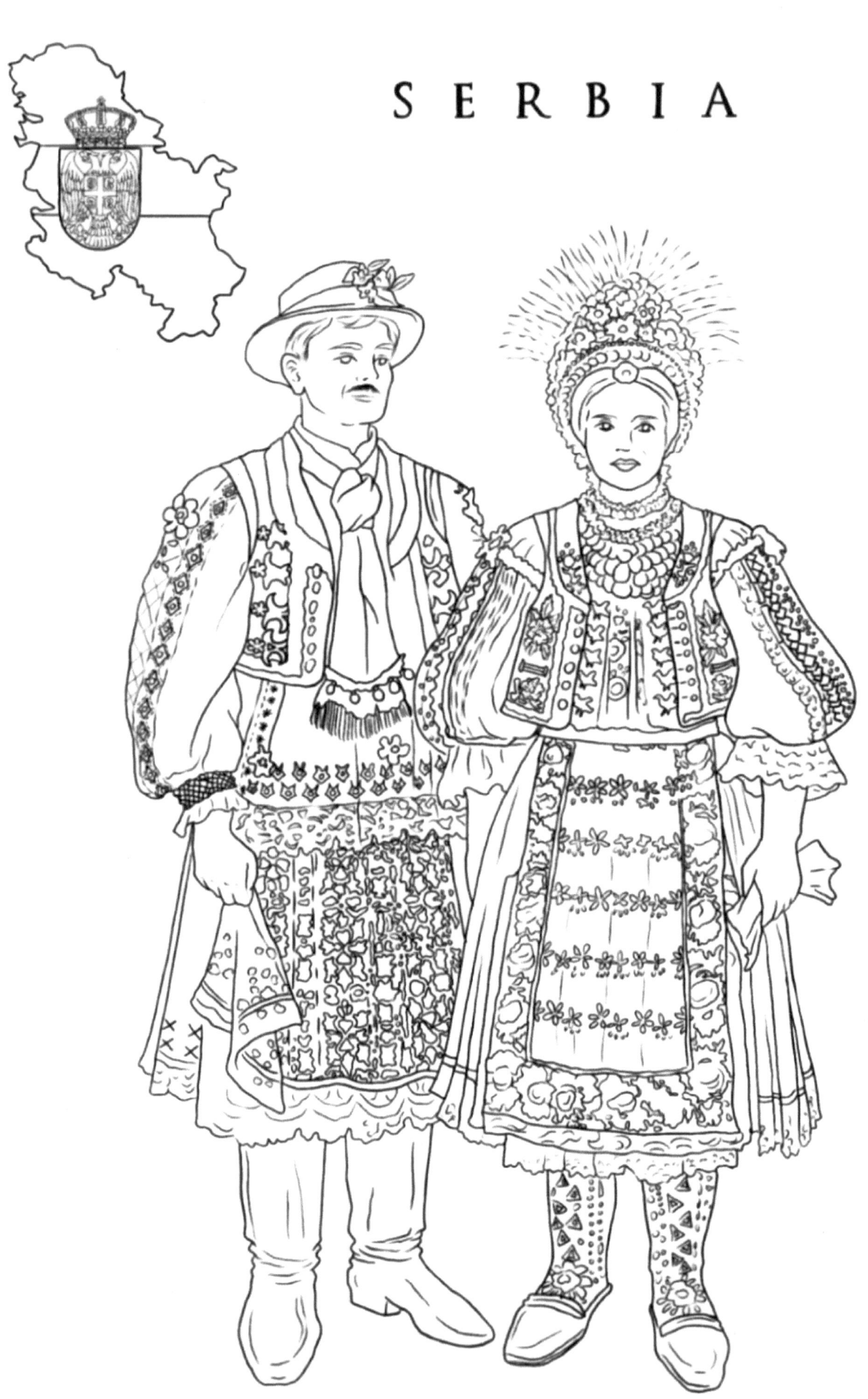

NATIVE AMERICANS

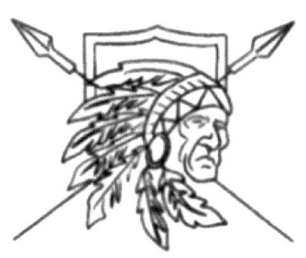

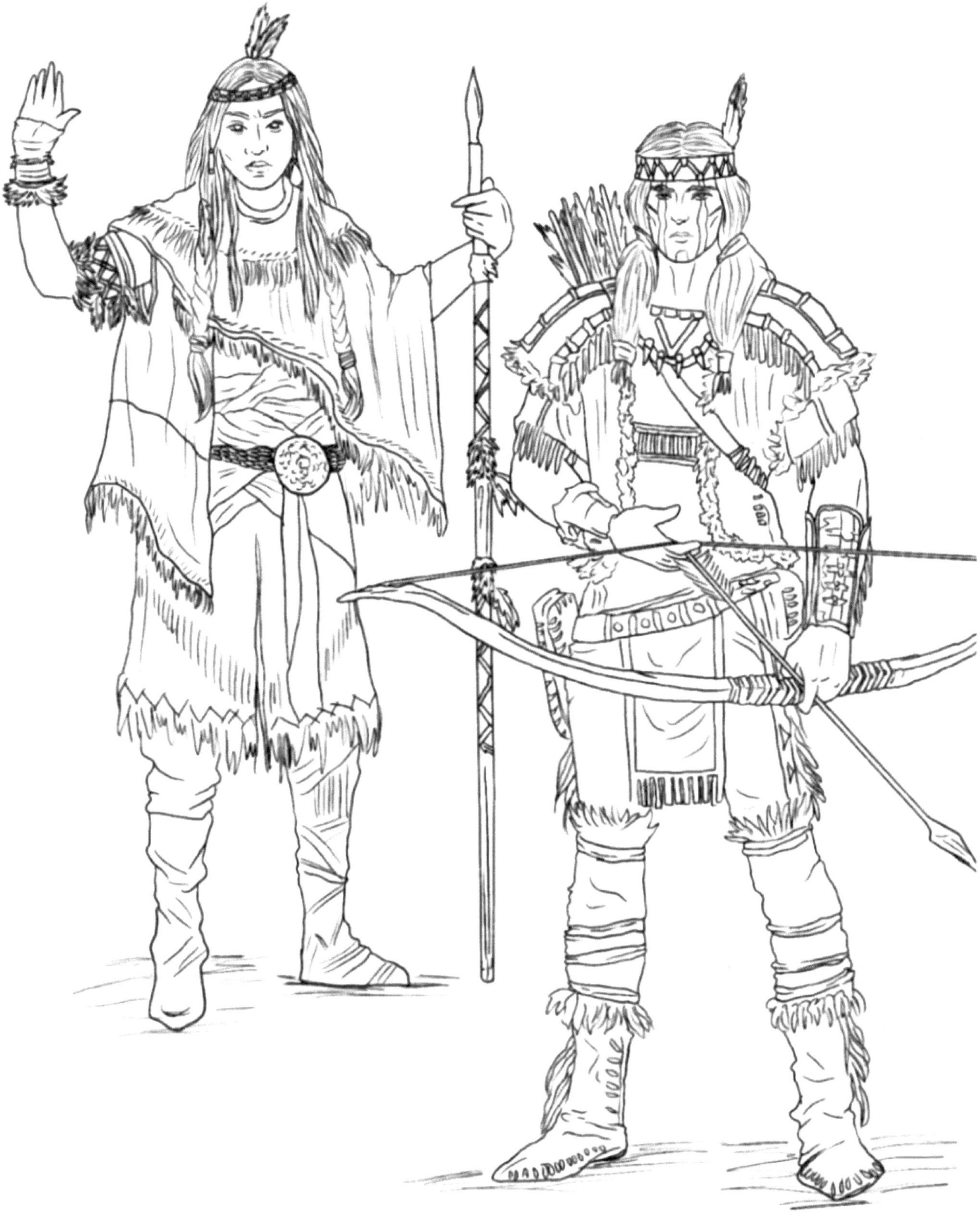

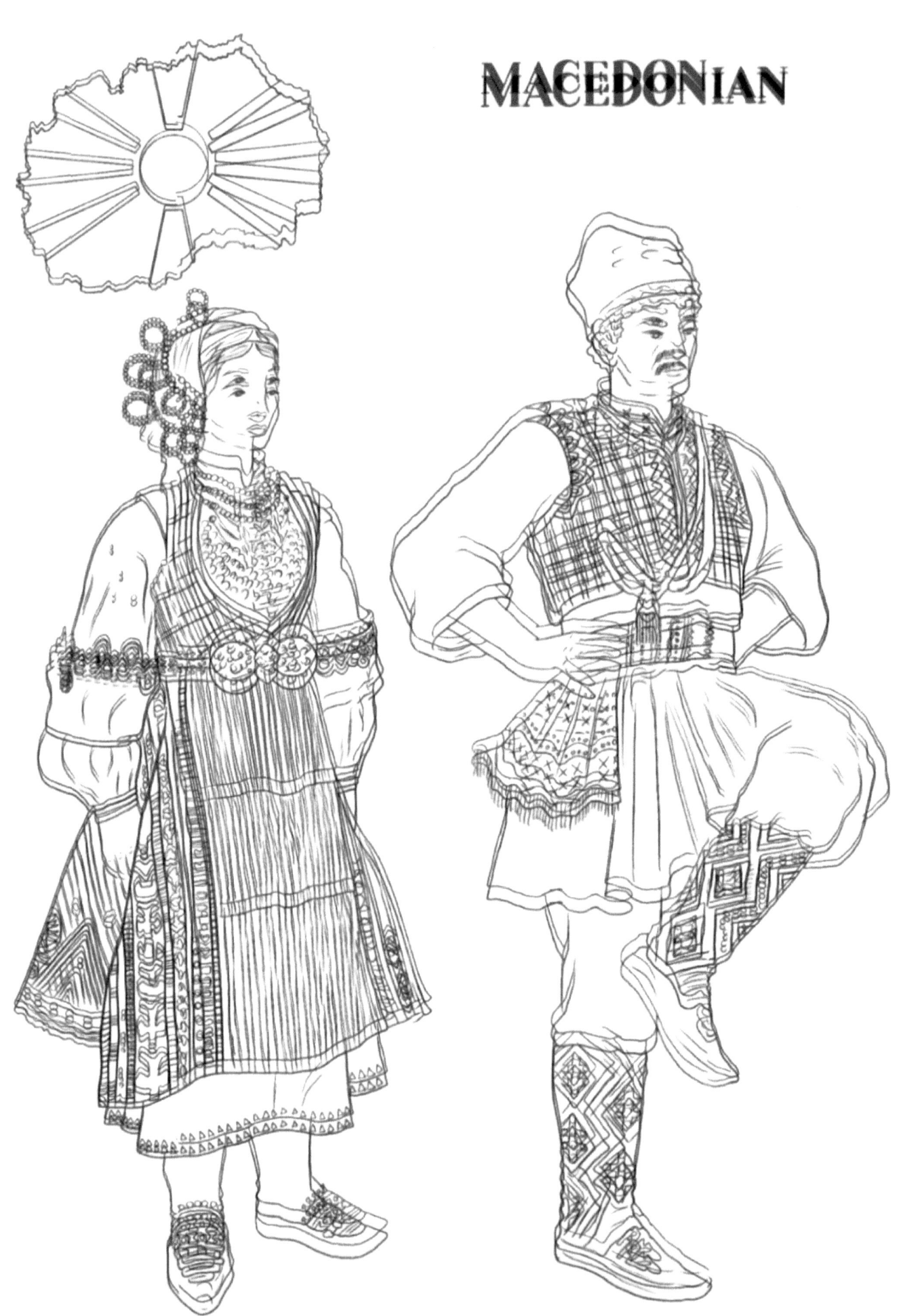

MACEDONIAN

UDMURTIA

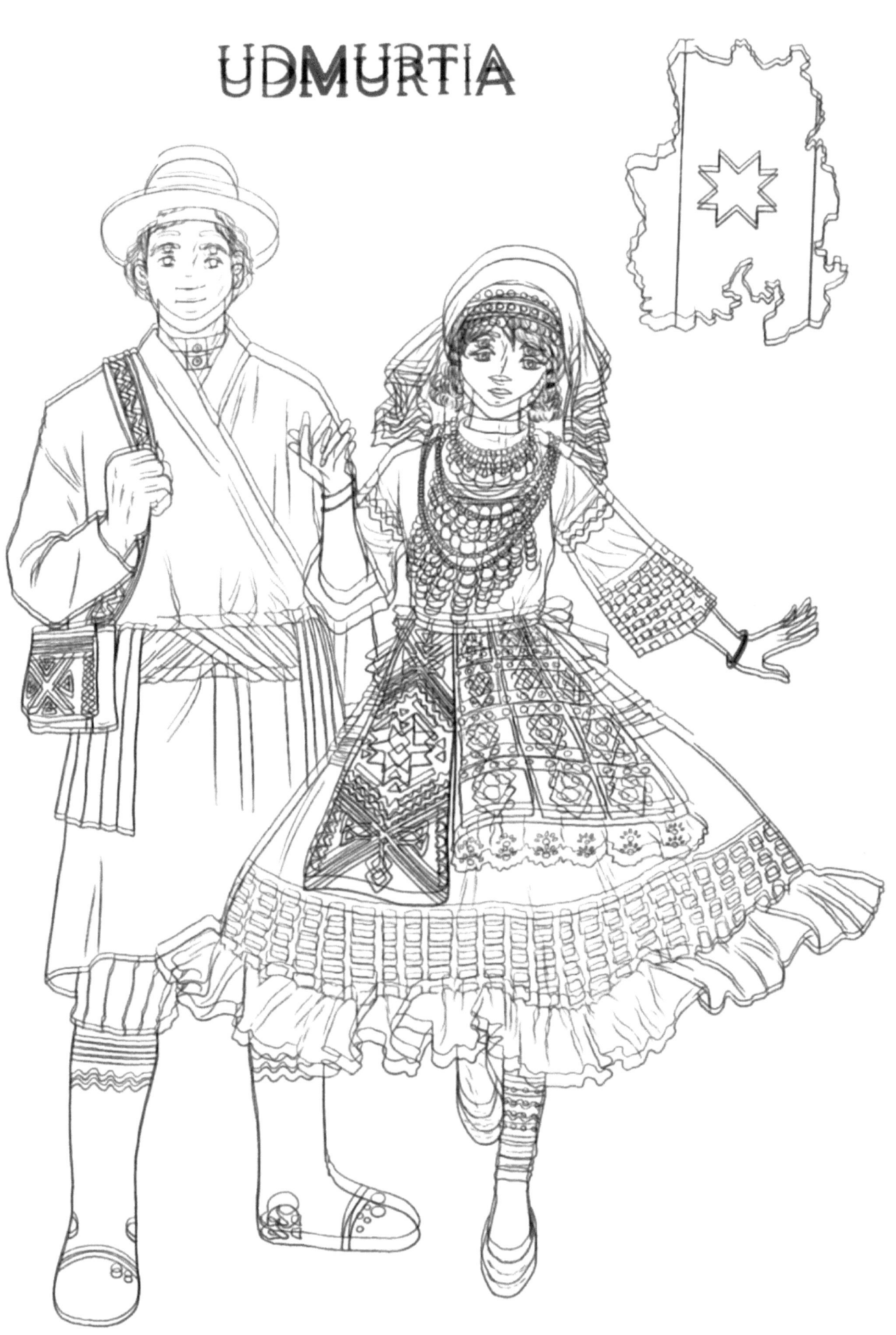

HUNGARY

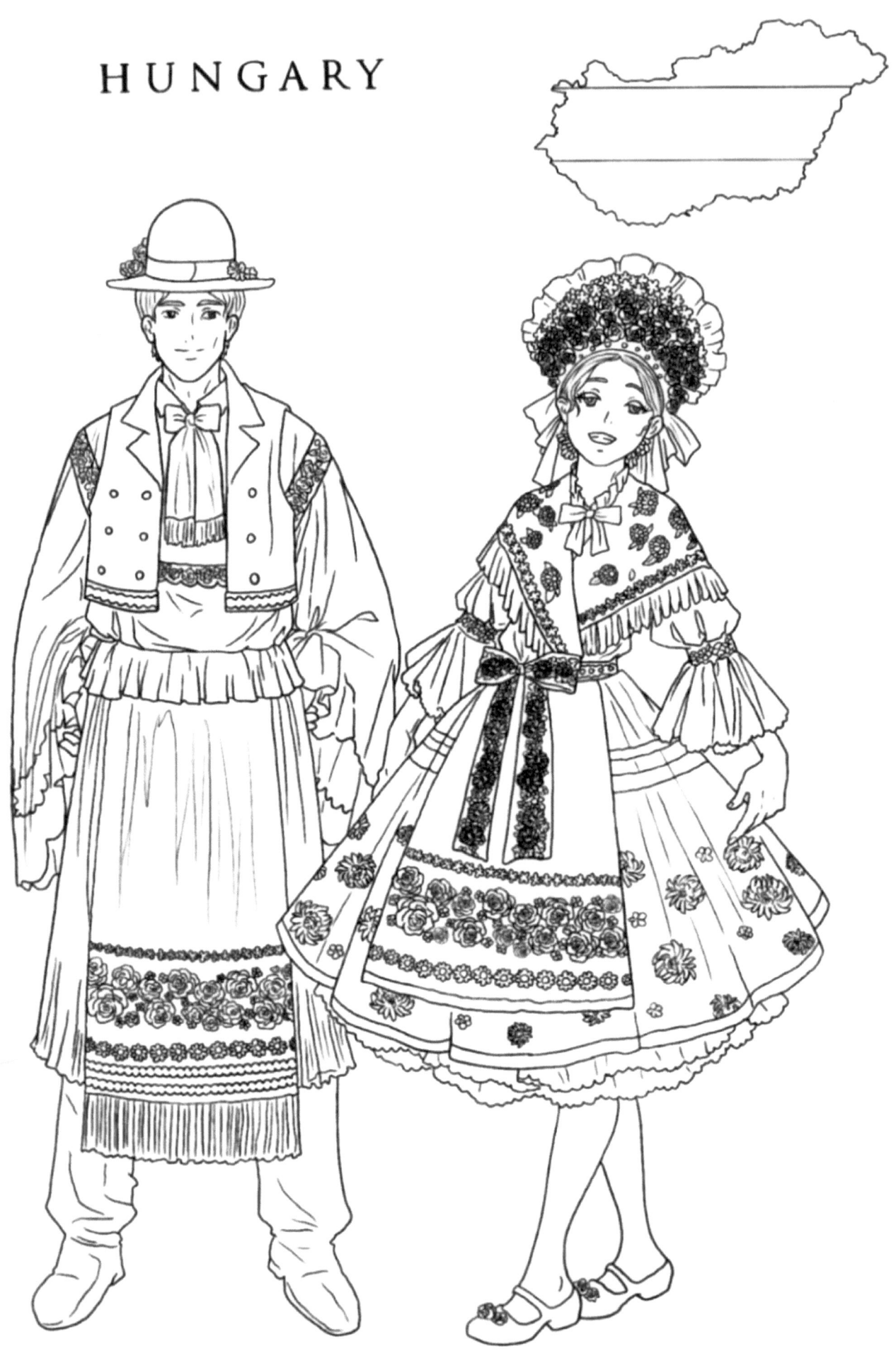

YUGOSLAVIA

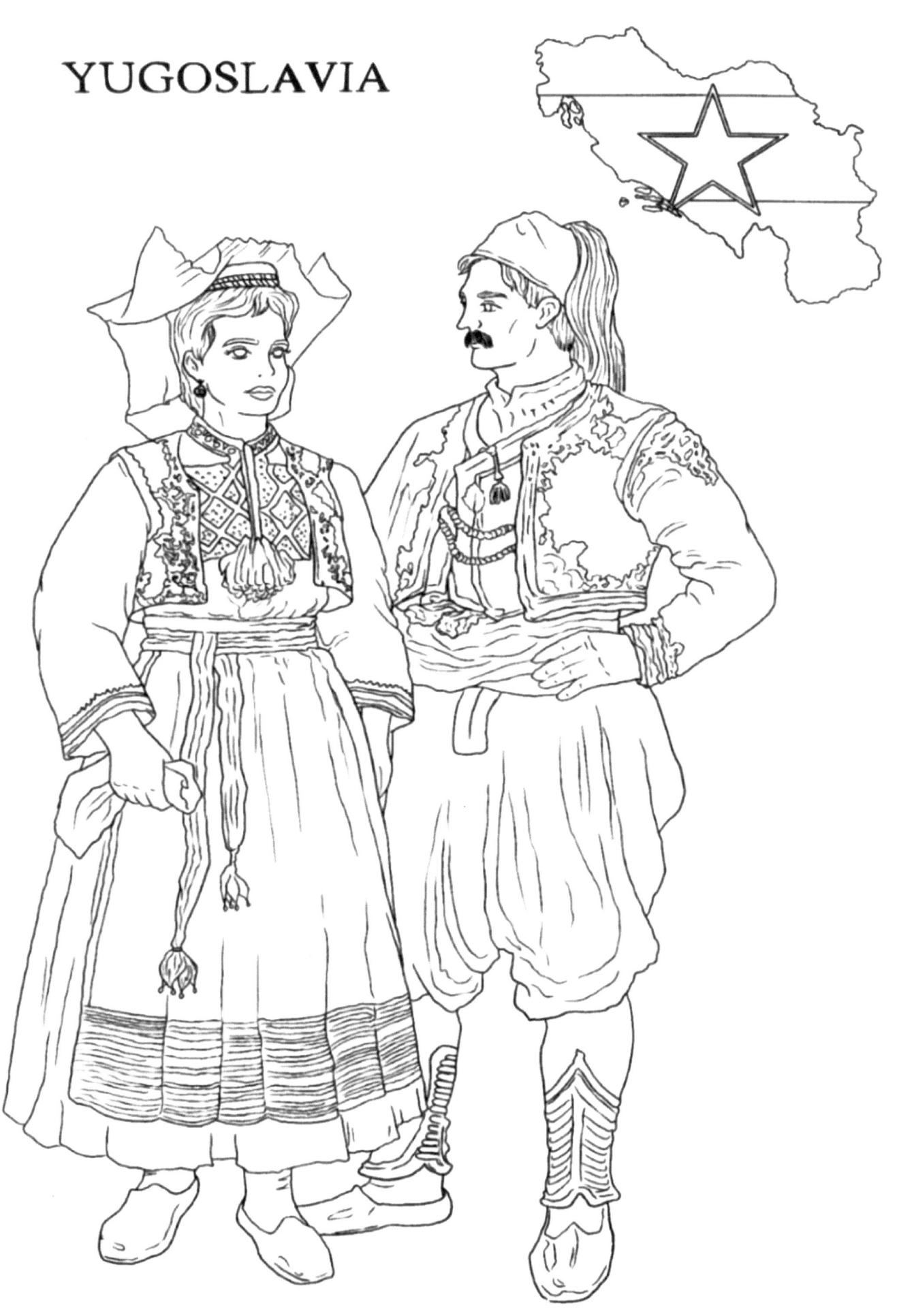

UKRAINE

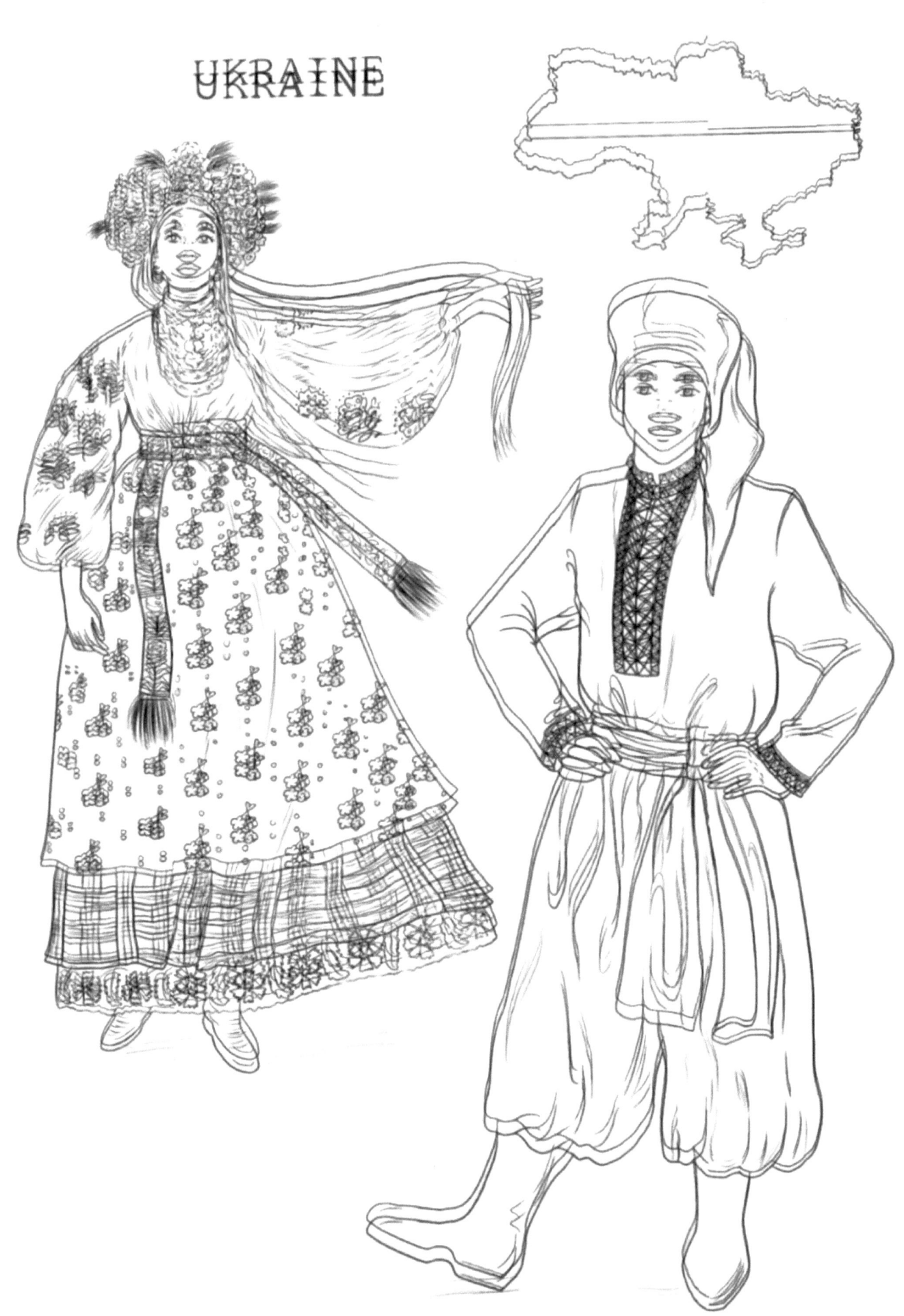

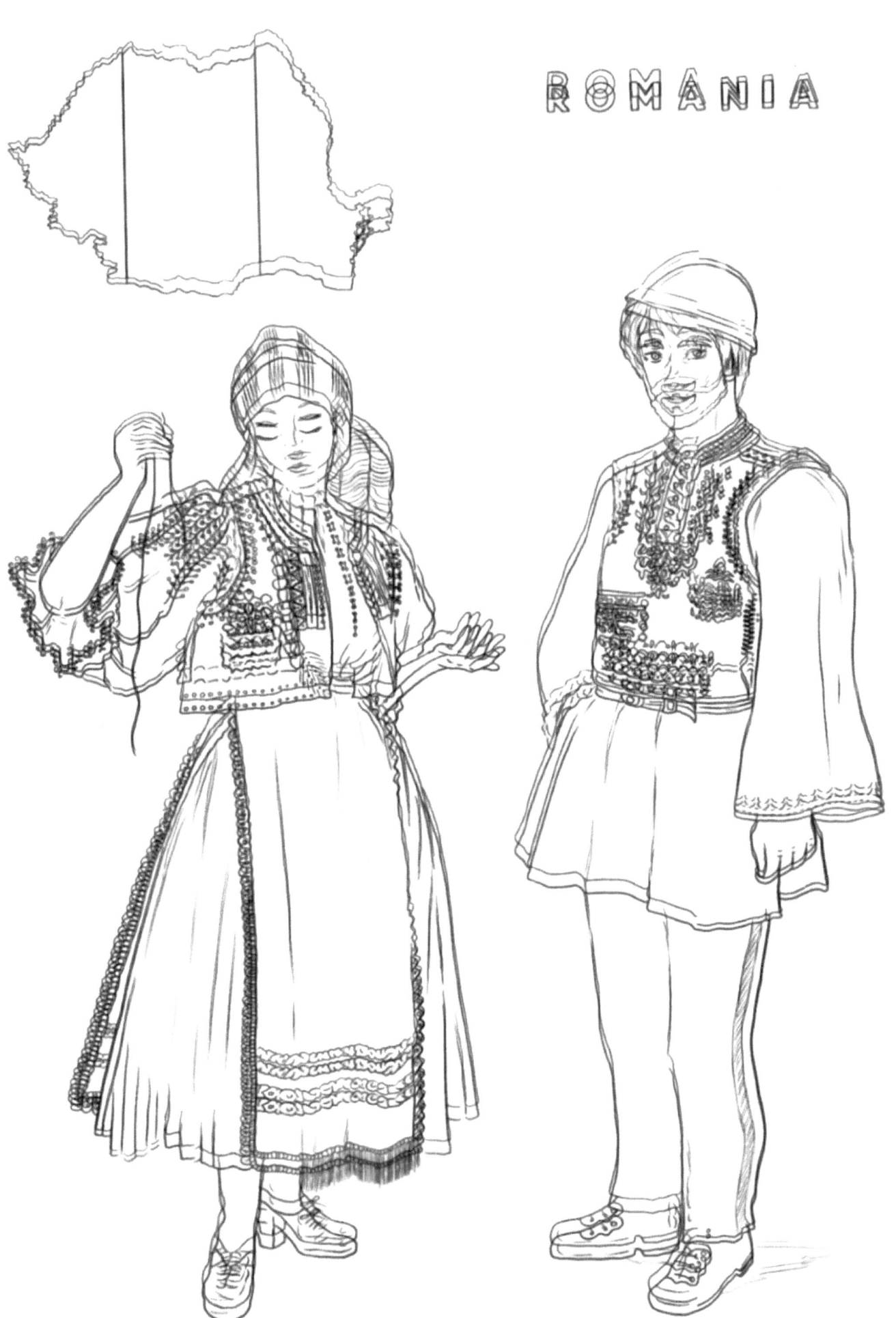

PALESTINE

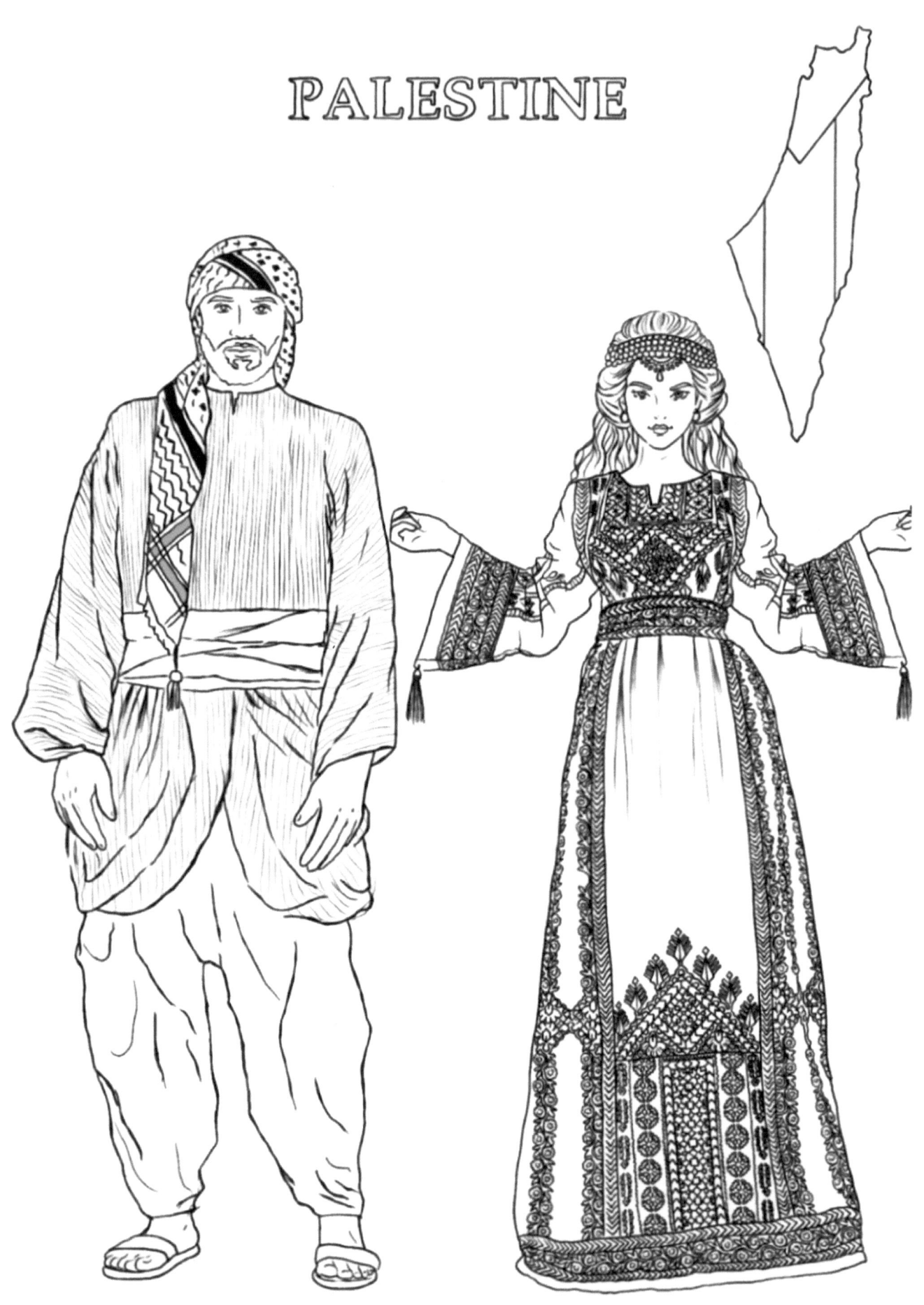

Ancient EGYPT

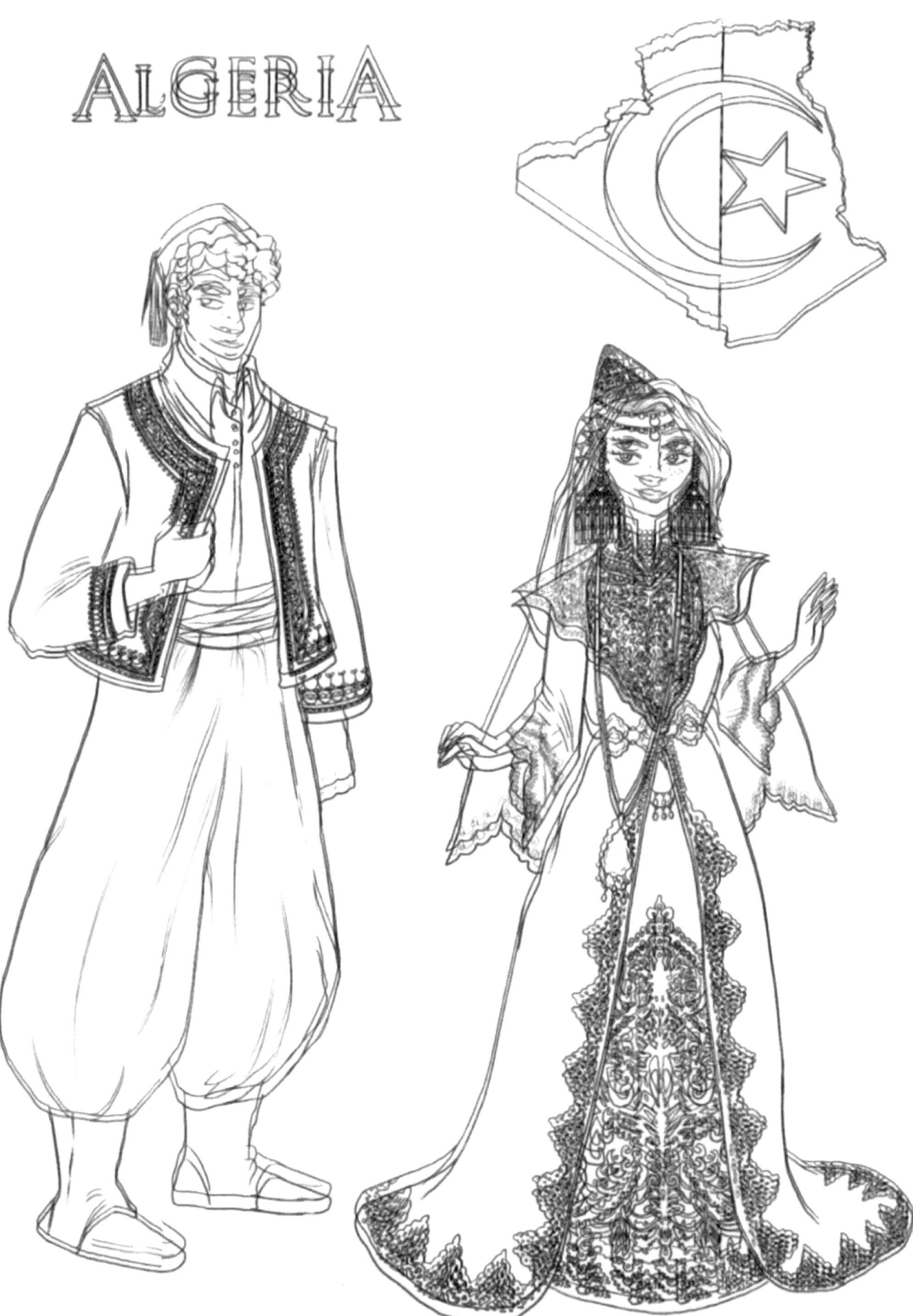

LATVIA

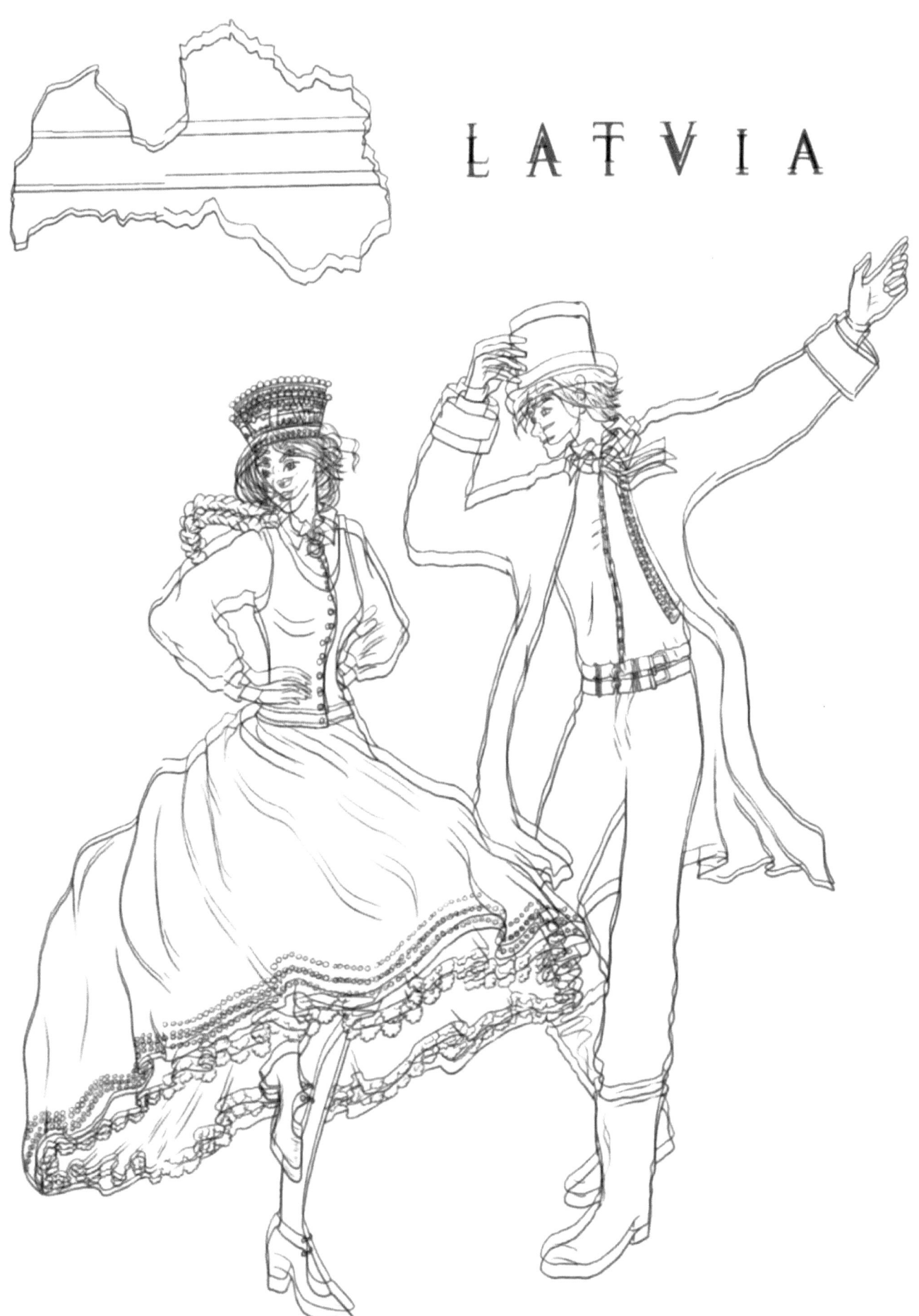

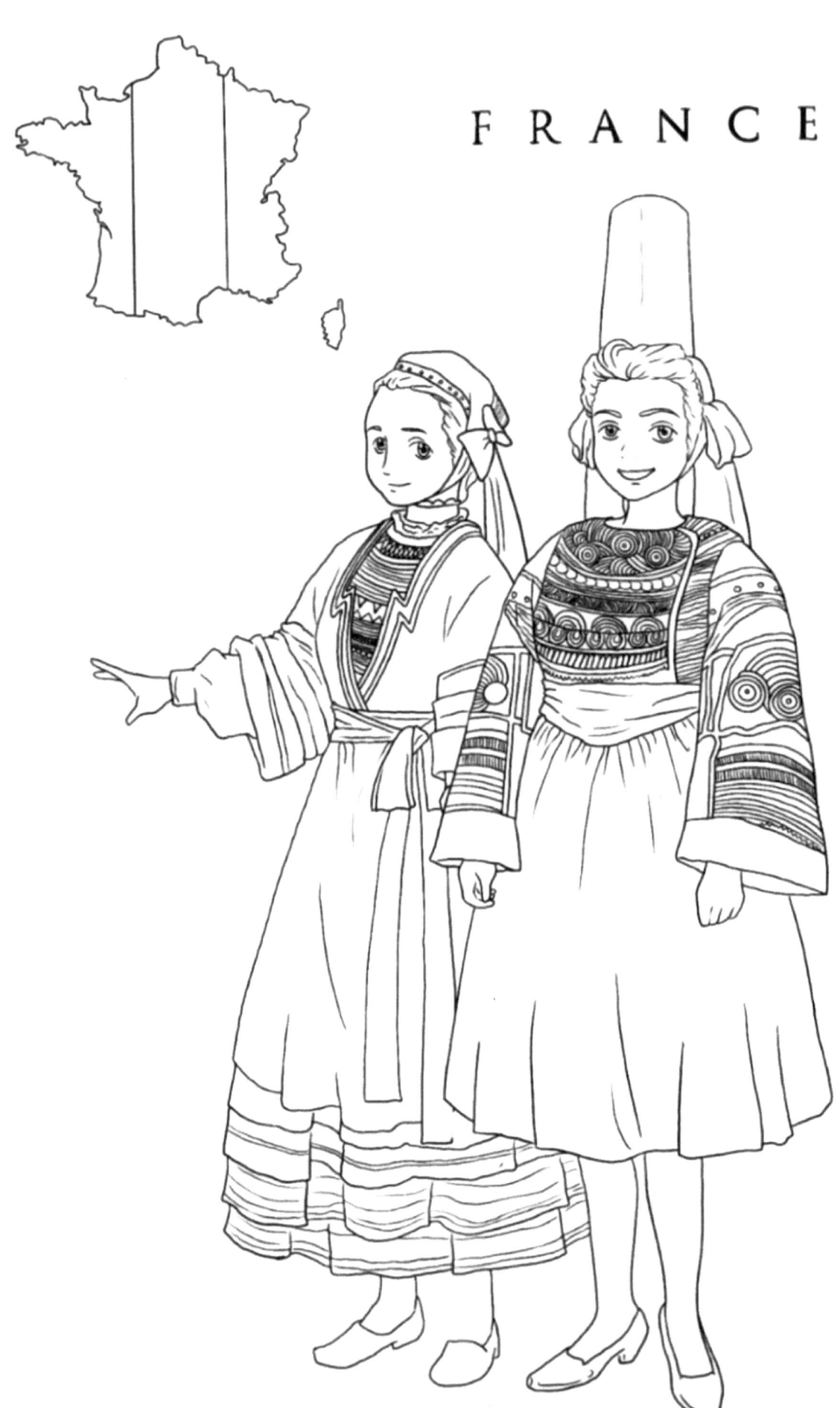

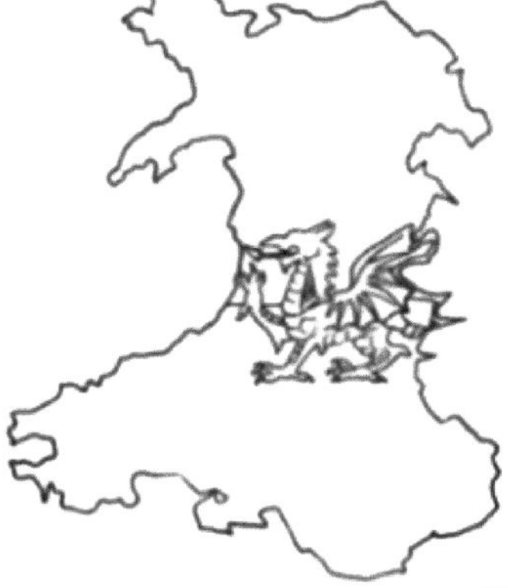

WALES

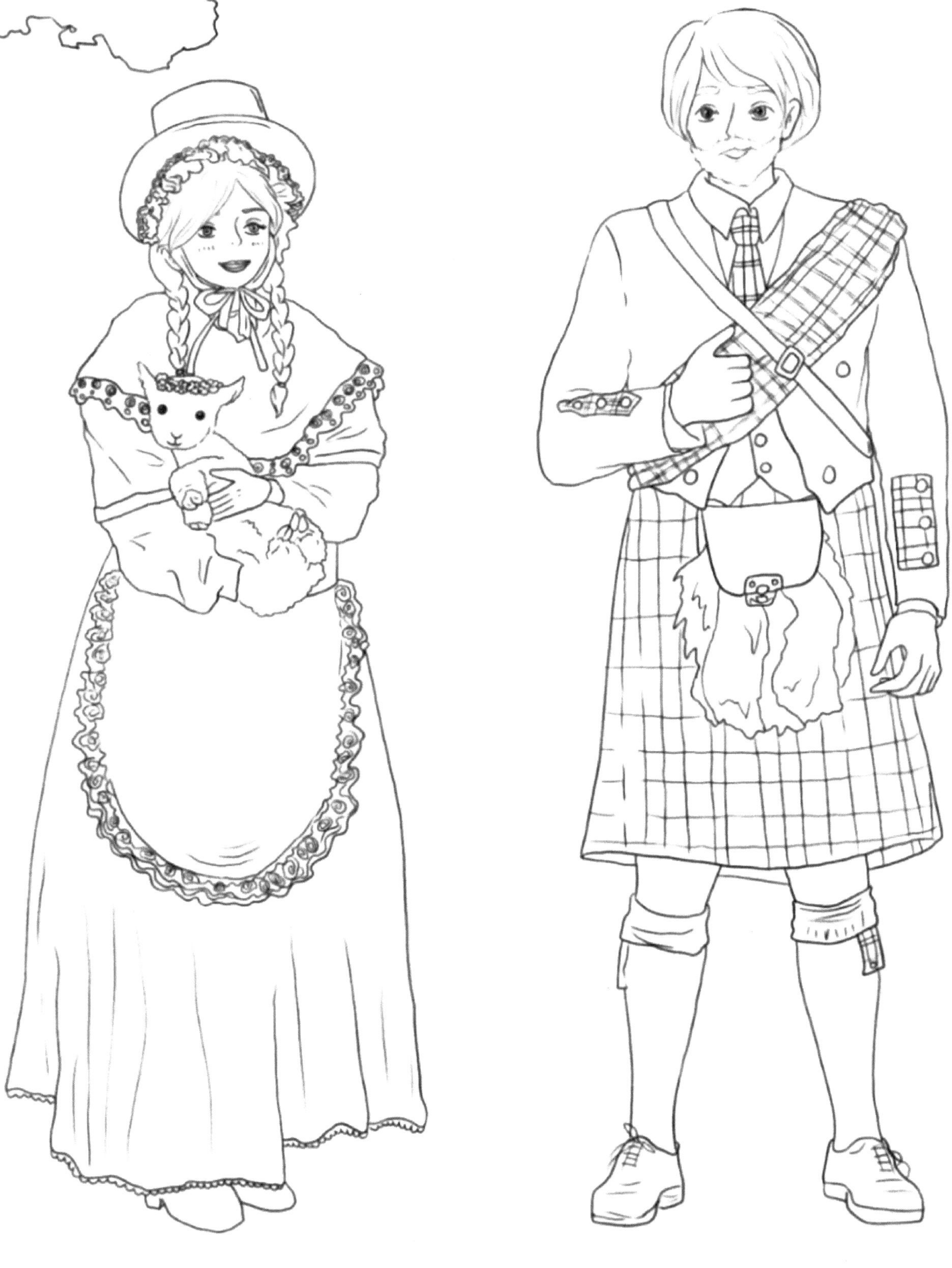

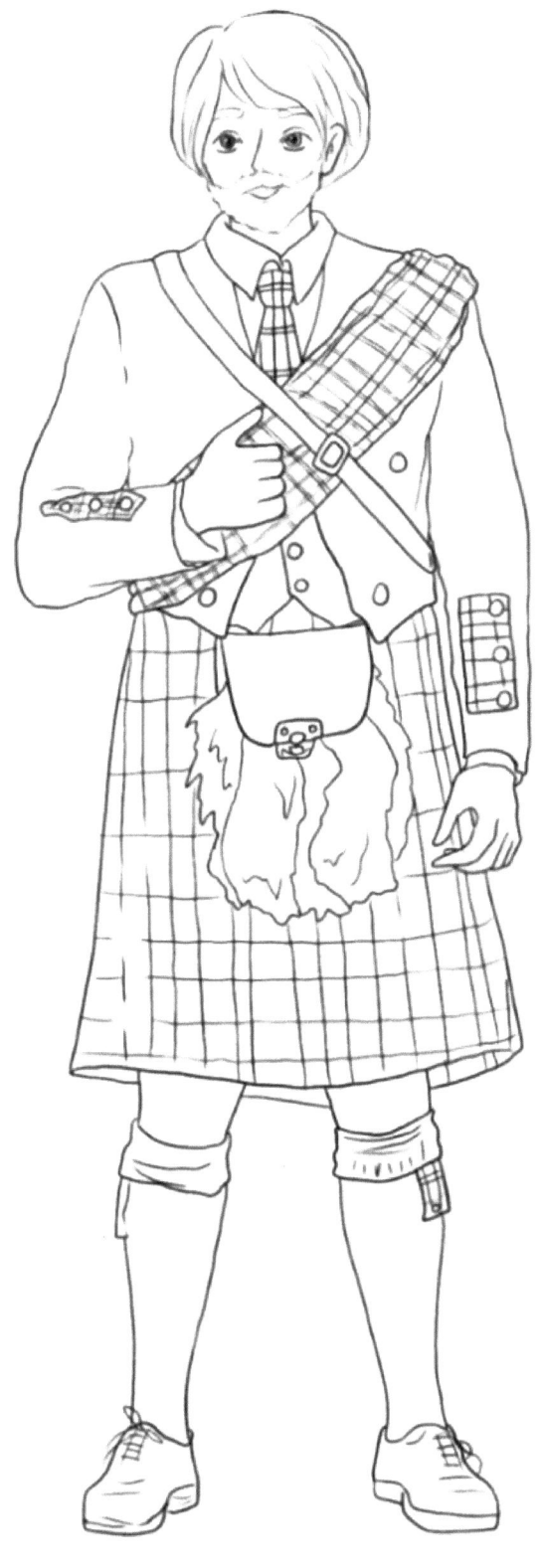

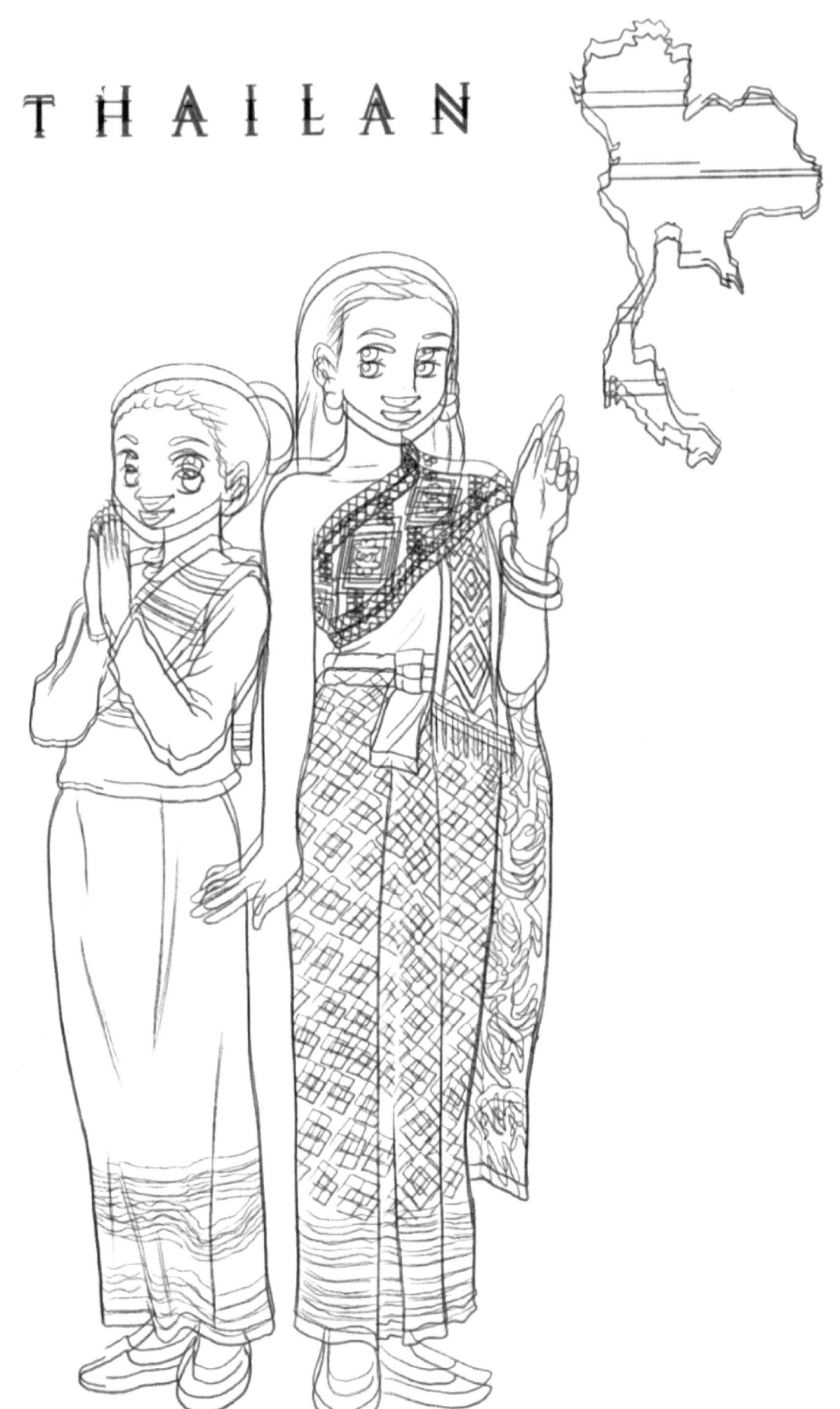

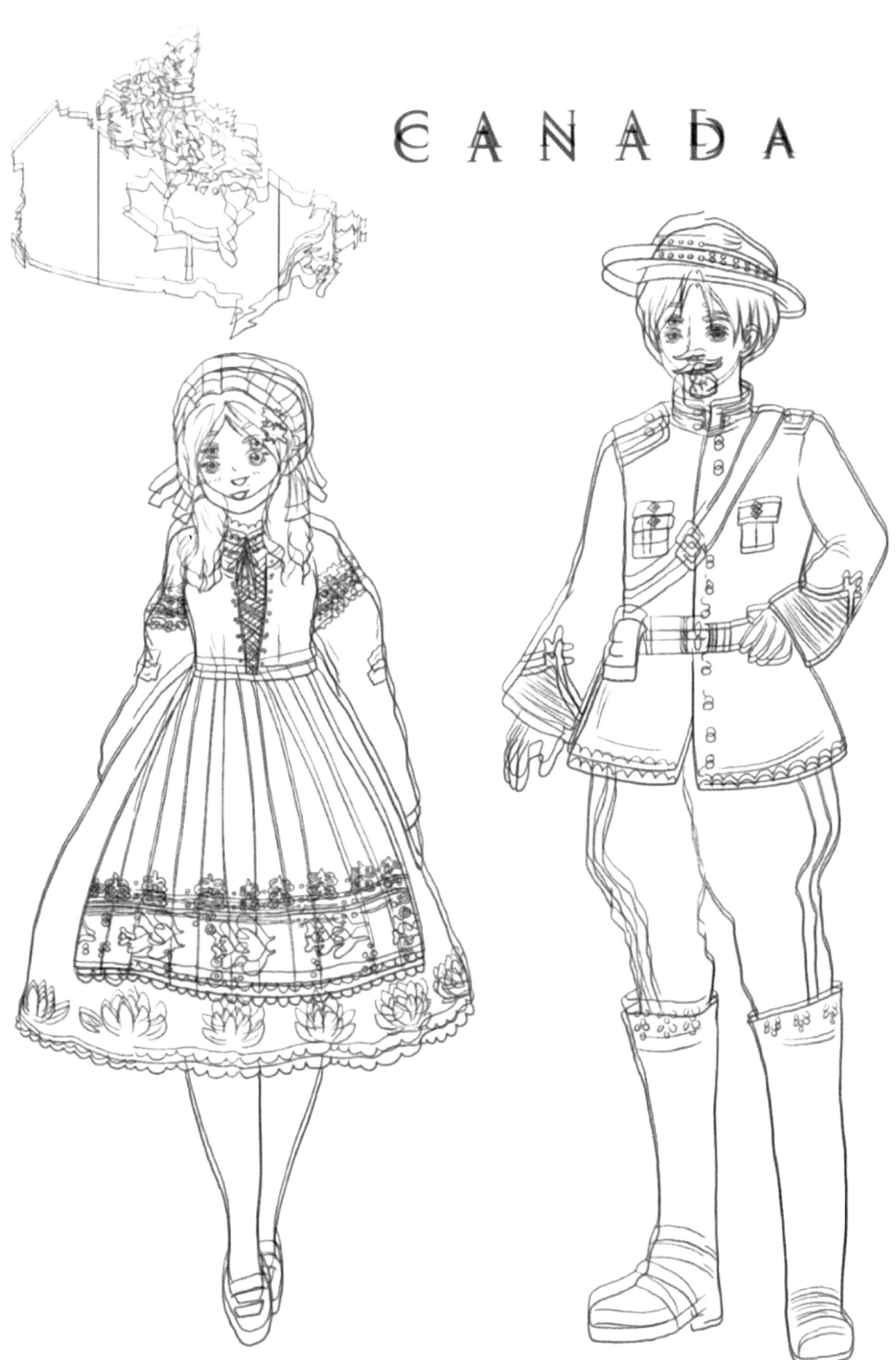

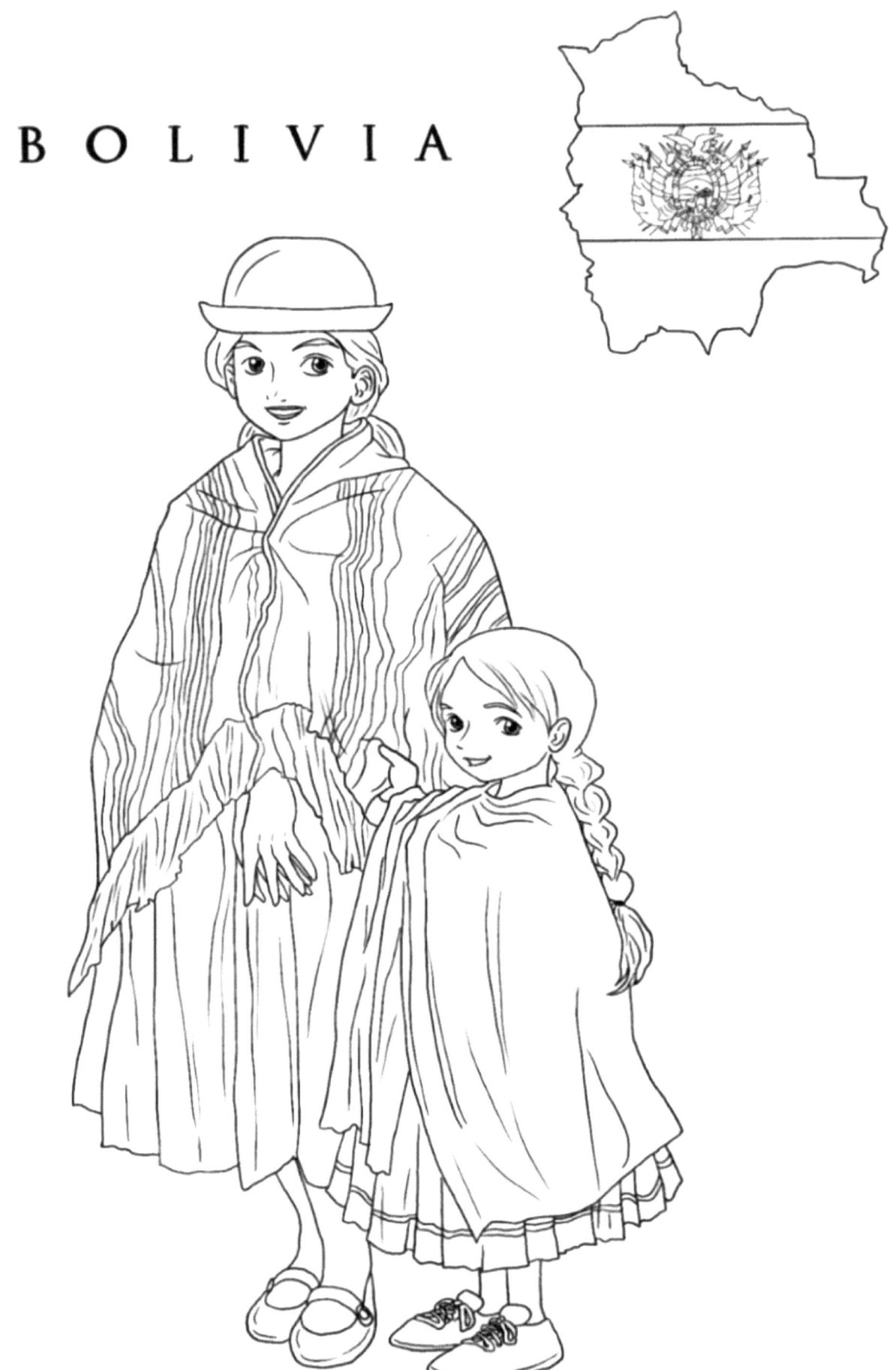

www.ingramcontent.com/pod-product-compliance
Lightning Source LLC
Chambersburg PA
CBHW051945210526
45473CB00006B/2386